bubblefacts...
ANCIENT EGYPT

Miles Kelly
PUBLISHING

First published in 2004 by
Miles Kelly Publishing Ltd
Bardfield Centre, Great Bardfield, Essex, CM7 4SL

Copyright © Miles Kelly Publishing Ltd 2004

2 4 6 8 10 9 7 5 3 1

Editorial Director:
Anne Marshall

Senior Editor:
Belinda Gallagher

Editorial Assistant:
Lisa Clayden

Designer:
Debbie Meekcoms

Cartoons:
Mark Davis

Production:
Estela Godoy

ISBN 1–84236–390–5

Printed in China

British Library Cataloguing-in-Publication Data
A catalogue record for this book is available from the British Library

Indexer: Jane Parker

www.mileskelly.net
info@mileskelly.net

Contents

Fancy pharaohs
leaders of Egypt

Rulers of ancient Egypt were called pharaohs. The word pharaoh means 'great house' and comes from the Egyptian word for palace – *per'ao*. The pharaoh was the most important and powerful person in the land and ordinary people believed he was a god.

Can you believe it?

Women courtiers wore hair cones made of animal fat scented with spices and herbs.

THIS FEATHER IS SO HEAVY!

I QUITE FANCY NAIL EXTENSIONS.

GUCCI, ARMANI...

The pharaoh was waited on hand and foot while people came to pay him tribute. They often gave gifts.

The pharaoh had many wives and he usually married a close female relative. He had lots of children!

The eldest son of the pharaoh became the next leader. Female pharaohs were not very common!

Classy Egyptians

who's who?

The ancient Egyptians were organized into upper, middle and lower classes. The royal family, government officials, priests, scribes and doctors made up the upper class. Traders, merchants and craftworkers were middle class. The biggest group of people – unskilled workers – made up the lower class.

Servants did everything in rich households – they looked after the children and cooked and cleaned.

Egyptians wanted servants in the afterlife! People were buried with models called shabtis, which were meant to come to life to look after their dead owner!

The ancient Egyptians were the first people to domesticate (tame) cats. They helped to keep households free of pests, such as mice. Cats gradually became associated with Bastet, goddess of musicians and dancers. It was against the law to harm a cat and pet cats were buried in their own cemetery when they died.

ONE FOR YOU, ONE FOR ME.

WHOOOSH!

STRAWBERRY PICKING'S EASIER...

GRRR!

Pets were popular and sometimes baboons were kept and trained to pick figs from trees!

Home sweet home

Egyptian style

Egyptian houses were made from mud bricks dried in the sun.

Mud from the River Nile was mixed with straw and pebbles to make it stronger. Tree trunks supported the flat roofs. Inside walls were plastered and painted. Wealthy Egyptians lived in large houses while a poorer family might live in a single room.

Many poor people lived in a crowded single room, but the rich had spacious villas with a walled garden.

Food was cooked in a clay oven or over an open fire. Most kitchens were equipped with a cylinder-shaped oven made from bricks of baked clay. Egyptians burned either charcoal or wood as fuel and cooked food in two-handled pottery saucepans.

Egyptians furnished their homes with wooden stools, chairs, tables, storage chests and carved beds. A low three- or four-legged footstool was one of the most popular items of furniture. Mats of woven reeds covered the floors.

The Egyptians ate with their fingers. Servants brought jugs of water so people could rinse their hands.

Baking and brewing
bread and beer!

Bread was the most important food in ancient Egypt. Grain was stored in huge granaries until it was needed. Ordinary Egyptians' favourite drink was beer. Models of brewers were even left in tombs to make sure the dead person had a plentiful supply of beer in the next world!

WHISTLE WHILE YOU... HIC... WORK!

THESE NEW PIZZA BASES ARE SELLING LIKE HOT CAKES!

ONE LARGE BLOOMER — ANYTHING ELSE MADAM?

A rough bread was made from wheat or barley. The gritty pieces often wore down people's teeth!

As well as beer, the Egyptians made wine, usually from grapes. After harvesting, the grapes were trodden by foot in a wine press, until every last drop of juice was squeezed out! The juice was then left in jars to ferment (turn into alcohol).

Beer made from barley was drunk by the poor. It was so thick it had to be strained before drinking.

Looking good!

Egyptian fashion

Egypt was a hot country so people wore cool, loose-fitting clothes. Noblewomen's dresses were made from the finest cloth with beads sewn onto it. Men wore robes or a piece of cloth worn like a kilt. Ordinary workers just wore a simple cloth tied at the waist.

Clothes were made of linen, a cloth spun from a plant called flax. Shoes were a luxury, loved by the rich!

Sandals were made from papyrus, a kind of reed. Rich people, courtiers and kings and queens wore padded leather sandals, but footwear was a luxury item, and most ordinary people walked around barefoot. Sometimes sandals were painted onto the feet of mummies!

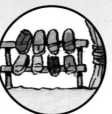

Lucky charms called amulets were also worn. They were supposed to protect the wearer from evil spirits and bring good luck. One of the most popular ones was the eye of the god Horus. It was meant to protect everything behind it. Children wore amulets shaped like fish to protect them from drowning in the River Nile.

Women wore long dresses while men wore kilt-like skirts. Wigs were popular with men and women!

Buying and selling

trade in Egypt

Egyptians did not use money to buy and sell goods. Instead they exchanged goods with other traders. Merchants visited the countries bordering the Mediterranean Sea as well as those lands to the south. The Egyptians offered gold, a kind of paper called papyrus, and cattle.

Can you believe it?

Fly swatters made from giraffe tails were a popular fashion item in ancient Egypt.

WHAT? I HAVE TO PAY?

WELL IT'S NOT FREE!

BUZZ! BUZZZ!

Egyptians traded food and goods such as linen and papyrus with Nubia, a land to the south of Egypt.

Most towns had a market and people took oil in huge pots, which they exchanged for food or cloth.

People could also buy pots and pans, animal skins, silver, copper – in fact, almost anything!

Down on the farm
a farmer's tale!

The farming year was divided into three seasons: the flood, the growing period and the harvest. Most people worked on the land, but between July and November the land was covered by flood waters. People went off to help build pyramids and royal palaces.

WHO DOES HE THINK HE IS?

YEAH — IF HE CRACKS THAT WHIP AGAIN...

CRACK!

Farmers used wooden ploughs pulled by oxen to prepare the soil. Seeds were planted by hand.

Wheat and barley were the two main crops. At harvest time, wooden sickles were used to cut the crop.

Farmers had to hand over part of their harvest as tax payment. It was given to the local temple.

A hard day's work

scribing away!

Scribes were very important people in ancient Egypt. These highly skilled men kept records of everything that happened from day to day. Craftworkers produced statues, furniture and other goods for the pharaoh. These workers sometimes had special villages built for them, especially those who worked on the pharaohs' tombs.

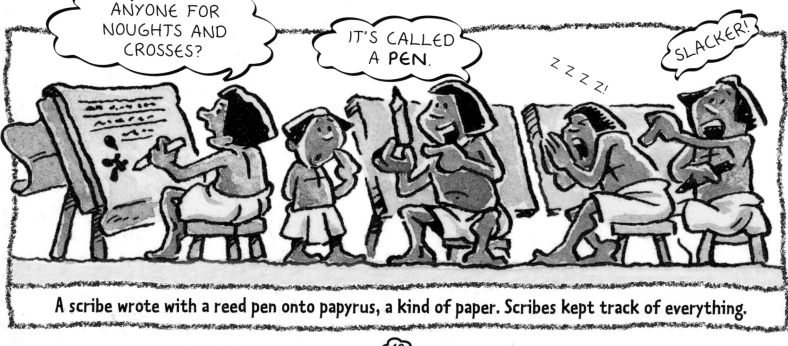

A scribe wrote with a reed pen onto papyrus, a kind of paper. Scribes kept track of everything.

Only the sons of scribes could undergo the strict scribe training, which began at about nine years of age. It took years to learn the hundreds of hieroglyphs (word pictures) that were used in writing.

IT'S AS EASY AS ABC!

HOW MANY STOOLS DOES ONE PHARAOH NEED?

THEY'RE PROBABLY FOR ALL THE WIVES HE'S GOT!

RIBBIT!

Craftworkers included carpenters, potters and jewellers. They worked mainly for the pharaoh.

Fun and games

hunting hippos

Hippo hunting was a dangerous but popular sport in ancient Egypt. Hunters in reed boats, armed only with spears and ropes, killed hippos in the waters of the Nile. In the desert, hunters chased lions, antelope, wild bulls, gazelles and hares. Birds were hunted with sticks shaped liked boomerangs.

Hippo hunting was reserved mainly for royalty. But an angry hippo could easily overturn a reed boat.

As well as hunting and sport, the Egyptians loved parties! A banquet was a real occasion as rich people could afford the best food and drink. There was music and dancing too – the ancient Egyptians knew how to enjoy themselves!

As well as lions and bulls, ducks were hunted. Whole families would attend a duck hunt.

Pyramid builders

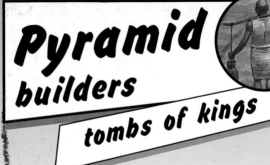

tombs of kings

The three pyramids at Giza were built for kings Khufu, Khafre and Menkaure. Pyramids were huge burial chambers. The biggest, the Great Pyramid, took more than 20 years to build. About 4000 stonemasons were needed to complete the job.

The huge stones had to be levered into exactly the right position. Up to two million blocks of stone could be used to make one pyramid. Teams of workers had to drag the stones up steep slopes.

The finished pyramids were given a white coating to protect the stones beneath

Wooden sledge for dragging the blocks of stone

The pyramids at Giza are more than 4500 years old. The Great Pyramid is about 140 metres high.

Steep ramps of earth were built to raise the stones onto the pyramid structure

Workers were supplied with water while working in the hot sun

The Sphinx, a stone statue, guards the pyramids. It has the body of a lion and the head of King Khafre.

Tombs and thieves

deep underground

GET ME A MUMMY!

From about 2150BC, the pharaohs were buried in tombs in the Valley of the Kings. The tombs were cut deep into rocks or underground. Over the years, robbers stole everything from these tombs – gold, silver, precious stones, furniture. Sometimes they even stole the body of the dead ruler.

IT'S LIKE ALADDIN'S CAVE.

THAT'S ALI BABA.

WHERE'S THE LIGHT SWITCH?

OPEN SESAME!

The entrance to the Valley of the Kings was guarded, but robbers broke into every tomb, except one.

can you believe it?

A handbook for tomb robbers, 'The Book of Buried Pearls', gave tips for sneaking past the spirits that guarded the dead!

All kinds of treasure was buried with a dead king in his tomb. It included gold, silver and precious stones along with personal belongings, jewellery and clothes. The tomb of Tutankhamun revealed the king's solid gold death mask.

I SAID DIG, YOU DOG!

OW!! WATCH WHERE YOU PUT THAT TORCH!

I'M SURE THERE'S A SWITCH HERE SOMEWHERE.

The tomb of Tutankhamun, the boy king, was discovered almost untouched in 1922.

Making mummies

wrap it up!

Mummies were dead bodies that had been preserved by priests.
The ancient Egyptians thought that the dead lived on in another world and that they would need their bodies in the afterlife. This meant that bodies were mummified, or dried out.

It took up to 70 days to prepare a body and only kings and nobles could afford the full treatment.

Making a mummy was a very skilled job. First of all, the internal organs such as the brain and lungs were removed. Then the body was covered in salts and left to dry for 40 days. The dried body was then stuffed with linen to help it keep its shape. Finally, the body was oiled and wrapped in layers of linen bandages.

When the body was ready for burial, the chief priest said prayers to help the dead person on their journey to the next world. He wore a jackal mask to represent Anubis – god of embalming (preparing bodies to be mummified). As jackals were often found near cemeteries, Anubis was given the form of a jackal.

GENTLY!

HOLY WATER? NO, IT'S JUST BOTTLED, I'M AFRAID!

SOB! WAIL!!

AATCHOOO!

I'M HAVING THE CAR!

The mummy of a pharaoh was sealed inside a stone coffin called a sarcophagus.

Gods and goddesses

Egyptian worship

The Egyptians worshipped more than 1000 different gods and goddesses. The most important god was Ra, the Sun god. People believed that he was swallowed each evening by the sky goddess, Nut. During the night Ra travelled through the underworld and was born again in the morning.

As well as Ra, Sobek, god of the Nile, was important. Crocodiles were kept in pools near his temples.

Thoth was moon god and gave people writing. Bastet was goddess of cats, musicians and dancers.

Anubis looked after the dead, and watched over them as their bodies were made into mummies.

Heroes of Egypt...
heroines too!

Rulers of ancient Egypt achieved great things. Ramses II built the famous rock temple at Abu Simbel and the Great Hall at Karnak. After his death nine other pharaohs were given his name. Queen Cleopatra was one of the last rulers of ancient Egypt. She married the Roman general Mark Antony but killed herself when the Romans conquered Egypt.

PUT YOUR FOOT DOWN!

CRACK!

I'M THE BOSS, I'LL DECIDE WHERE IT GOES!

IT'S ME, QUEEN HAT!

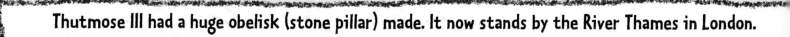

Thutmose III had a huge obelisk (stone pillar) made. It now stands by the River Thames in London.

can you believe it?

Soldiers who fought bravely in battle were given golden fly medals for 'buzzing' the enemy so successfully!

Queen Hatsheput was often shown wearing men's clothing and a false beard. She was the wife of Thutmose II. On his death, Hatsheput took the title of pharaoh and adopted the royal symbols of the double crown, the crook, the flail (whip) – and also the ceremonial beard!

LOOK, CLEO, WHAT ABOUT CAESAR? IT'S ME OR HIM!

IT'S MY TREASURE!

I'M NOT CARRYING THIS ALL THE WAY TO LONDON...

Perhaps the most famous pharaoh is Tutankhamun, and his tomb of fabulous treasure.

Index